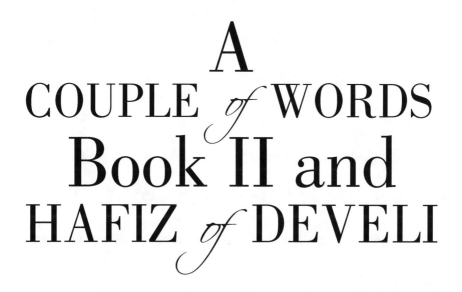

A
COUPLE *of* WORDS
Book II and
HAFIZ *of* DEVELI

H. I. Mavioglu

iUniverse LLC
Bloomington

A COUPLE OF WORDS BOOK II AND HAFIZ OF DEVELI

iUniverse books may be ordered through booksellers or by contacting:

iUniverse LLC
1663 Liberty Drive
Bloomington, IN 47403
www.iuniverse.com
1-800-Authors (1-800-288-4677)

ISBN: 978-1-4917-1932-9 (sc)
ISBN: 978-1-4917-1933-6 (e)

Printed in the United States of America.

iUniverse rev. date: 12/19/2013

Contents

A Couple Of Words

Hafiz of Develi

Acknowledgement

A poet is not a scribe but an idler who observes, feels and reflects what there may be in his private world. In this book characters, historical events, and geographic locations are fictitious. They may be parallel to reality but are not the reality itself.

A poet's most valued material is the word, and there is not a single word that has not been used before but many have not been heard before. A poet chooses his words from a vast ocean of words and pairs them according to their vowels and consonants and tunes them together to make them sing. Even then, a poet's agony is not over, for time warps words' meanings and silences their songs.

I am grateful for many places that I have been and for many souls I have met.

These poems came to me at their chosen moment and I celebrated their birth with following kindred spirits: Suzan Barnes, Andrea Cook, Grace Long, Christa Richardson, Margaret Johnson, Richard Meister Jr., Patricia Pfeiffer, Steven Hughes, Dr. N.H.I 'Hodja" Basho, Kirk Firestone and Joyce, Nelsilhan and Kurt Mavioglu.

A Couple Of Words

As a Recipient I Know my Rights

I

I will not be discouraged by a little lump
In my lung for my God is always on my side.
I don't have to worry about my failing pump;
Because, another heart, He can provide.

Hurry doctor! My transplant must not be delayed,
And later on, submit my bills to medicaid.

II

Although bad things happen to us by chance alone,
The Devil we find guilty and God we acquit.
As a judge, we judge unjustly and we condone
Selfishness to use others for our benefit.

We say, "A matched heart from a donor is our prayer
Knowing that no one has an extra heart to spare."

C'Est La Vie

I

Young lovers instinctively love with zeal,
Being charmed by love, they love what they feel.
When each lover starts to feel like a winner,
They nurture their love near to ideal.

II

When we met, I also was a beginner.
Heart said, "Talk of true love, open your inner
Space; let her in." Mind said, "Discretion! She
Is not yet primed for a candlelight dinner."

III

We attended the Houston Symphony.
It was an event to hear and to see
Sir Thomas Beecham. I said, "No encore!"
For a song and a verse were haunting me.

"My eyes search all over for you,
To cherish and to adore you.
This world flaunts its girls as it turns,
Yet never can I ignore you."

"My flaming heart is a crater; it burns.
Even when you are near me, my heart yearns."
Finally, a lover lays down his own rule;
Not by grabbing, but by giving he earns.

IV

You were the risk-taker; so, left your school
To wear the white bridal gown and the tulle.
In due time, you gave birth to our first-born;
Before long, found yourself in Istanbul.

We entered Istanbul through the time worn
Gate, passed Roman aqueducts which stand lorn
At the edge of the old town, and we could see
The new town just beyond the Golden Horn.

Istanbul preserves its identity
As lovers' bliss; broken hearts' remedy.
The city no longer needs its old wall,
But ghosts on the wall chant their rhapsody.

V

I was happy to be home after all,
For you there was nobody there to call.
On the Bosphorus, we found a spot
But no one there could grasp your Texas drawl.

A family was not all that you got,
Soon Ortakoy became your Camelot.
There folks liked you for being outgoing,
And embraced you as a compatriot.

I could not believe that I could grow wing
To spread over you like a fairy king.
Soon you began to talk just as a tot,
And with each word you were triumphing.

Since you were not a natural diglot,
You developed other skills to sense what
Was on people's mind; without uttering
A single word you could solve any plot.

With our combined strengths, we were channeling
A deep channel in life, and fashioning
A new lifestyle fit for us to pursue,
And without our help, years were galloping.

You cared for grandma when she had the flu.
"Turkish girls wouldn't give such care for you,"
My aunt told my grandma. I chimed in,
"She can do things that other girls can't do."

VI

My aunt used to say while patting my chin,
"Be kind to her! She is missing her kin.
Surely, she is willing to sacrifice;
Her stand against longing is wearing thin."

VII

When one does not know the answer, one tries.
We went south in search of a paradise:
We liked the beaches, but ignored the clock,
And I gazed into our world through your eyes.

We followed the coast and reached Antioch.
The motel occupied a city block.
Blooms of passionflowers were purplish blue.
Who cared if our bed was hard as a rock.

Then the morning sickness was the first clue.
Soon after, you started to eat for two,
And all signs added up to an addition
To our tribe; and our dreams were coming true.

Together we formed a firm coalition,
And joined forces to shorten the transition
Period of moving. We were to land
In the U.S.A. before parturition.

VIII

While moving, one must avoid the quicksand
Of sentimentality, yet I planned
To take a fig sapling as a keepsake.
Though a smuggled seedling is contraband.

I found Isa's nursery by the lake.
In that place there was nothing false or fake.
I told old Isa what was on my mind.
He said, "Think son! It might be a mistake!

"A tree is no different than mankind.
Wherever it is taken, it must find
Neighbors who'll stand by it for friendship's sake,
For it to thrive without lagging behind.

"For a sapling everything is at stake.
I will prune any useless bulk or flake,
For a tree should not carry surplusage
That either can pull to pieces or break."

IX

America became my anchorage,
But I acquired no special privilege.
To blend, a newcomer must know the score,
And must keep holding to his heritage.

Getting a job was not an irksome chore.
The money trickled; though it did not pour.
We earned our daily bread right from day one;
Still, several fields were left to explore.

Our hard decision making days were gone,
Soon after you gave birth to our firstborn son,
We felt that no one else was more blessed than
Us between El Paso and Galveston.

We devised an uncomplicated plan
To grow together as one wife, one man,
One daughter and one son; we tried to blaze
A trail, barely wide enough, for our clan.

X

Then our thriving toddler son's sunny days
Were over, for a dark cloud cast a haze.
Not by choice but by an unforeseen twist
In the road, we ended up in a maze.

XI

When the fate coils to strike, no one can frist,
Much less to stop it, and no casuist
Can convince us that there's an intricate
Reason for the suffering to exist.

A tortured family's immediate
Reaction is to feel disconsolate,
And think that nothing can stop their dismay.
Then they search for a power to submit.

As we were occupied with everyday
Living, had no time for "what went astray?"
We had nothing to reject or to claim,
And stopped being the hunter or the prey.

We looked at the chaos with a new frame
Of mind, saw order though it stayed the same.
We grew perceptive and did comprehend
That fate is always ahead of the game.

XII

When kids were grown, you had one thing to mend,
There was unfinished college to contend.
I was your partner not just your roommate.
Your grit and hard work paid well to the end.

Flood of college work could not inundate
To drown your resolve nor could it frustrate.
You kept your composure and elegance,
And banked enough credits to graduate.

XIII

Our son wandered as if he were in a trance.
We followed him; he taught us acceptance.
We were certain he had nothing to tell,
Through his silence, he taught us tolerance.

XIV

For a while, the fig missed its native dell,
Still one must grow wherever one might dwell.
A tenacious tree that wants to thrive cleaves
To life itself with every living cell.

The fig is full-grown now; it interweaves
Its twisted branches all around the eaves.
After pruning it provides healthy shoots,
And pumps up its milky sap to its leaves.

Season after season, smoky air soots
Its leaves; it kisses the ground for its fruits,
Yet fierce winds can't uproot it with one fell
Swoop for it's firmly anchored by tough twin roots.

XV

When the kids were young our daughter was our belle,
But our son was an imp whom none could quell.
Since everything in life is relative
To something else, now they're doing quite well.

XVI

Since You know their sizes, why do You sieve?
The fine or the course is blessed when You give!
You're the Giver of Life none can deny.
But shall I know Your reasons while I live?

XVII

I carefully developed and streamlined my
Plan but the fate clipped its wings as it went by.
I devised another scenario
For life to revise and to modify.

XVIII

With their burdens, folks wandered to and fro,
But found no place to deposit their woe.
To trade their plights, they went to the bazaar
But each returned home with his ills in tow.

XIX

A peaceful pasture is never a far
Journey from the abhorrent abattoir.
Cycling of the sun, the rain, or the drought
Reshape and style us into what we are.

XX

May our days yield more of faith, less of doubt.
May we provide some shade for a parched sprout.
May we move forward with full energy,
And keep going till our engine conks out.

XXI

May our good thoughts flow through telepathy.
For each ill, may there be a remedy.
When our plans go awry, may we dismiss
The whys and hows by saying c'est la vie.

XXII

Before I sink deep into the abyss
Of the unknown, I solemnly swear this:
Fine details of our love I won't reveal
For my tight lips are sealed with your warm kiss.

Life Thrives on the Human Voice

I

As years slip by they don't steal everything.
They've snitched Beth's songs but left her things behind.
Still the ghost of her voice keeps echoing,
For they're determined to stay in my mind.

II

One day, I felt as if the world grew mute.
Although, I could hear the love songs of birds.
Then I realized there's no substitute,
For the melody of the spoken words.

III

The phone rang. A voice said, "I'm Monica,
I'll pick them up, if you've things to donate
To the Volunteers of America."
I've none, yet your call I appreciate.

IV

Without the human voice, I can't exist.
Kindly keep my name on your calling list.

A Lasting Line

I don't let my fancies get ahead of myself.
I don't worry if sales of my books lag behind,
Since I know they're doomed to collect dust on a shelf
It's hoped that a line may live on in someone's mind.

I Must Be Blessed for
I'm Given a Space

I

I hiked through foothills and by fertile farms,
Then camped in a meadow by a calm lake.
As a viper sped without legs or arms.
I mused about the success of the snake.

II

I observed a nearby appearing star.
Although, its distance from me is light-years;
In this cosmos nothing is insular.
All things evolve but nothing disappears.

III

I said, "This world is so vast, I'm so small,
Though I must count, for I'm assigned a space.
The meaning of life means the same for all,
If they could learn how to love and embrace.

IV

"To do something worthwhile life is too brief.
I doubt if it is even worth a try.
Though, All short term ventures don't come to grief;
Weeks are the life span for a butterfly.

V

"In this world I prize my free space the most.
Whether He hears or not, thanks to my Host."

Fused Feelings

I

You allured me with your beauty and grace.
Through your feelings, you taught me how to feel.
I welcomed you into my inner space,
Without questioning if your love was real.

I cannot foresee what each new moon brings;
Yet I feel the sting of Cupid's arrow.
As I fly high on love's whimsical wings,
I set my course by following your glow.

When I was alone, too vast was this world,
When we were together stars danced nearby.
With a zephyr our furled sails unfurled,
We sailed on calm sea under a blue sky.

Together we created our dreamland,
In there, happiness had no boundary.
We attuned our ears to the same waveband;
I heard true love songs as you sang to me.

Each day we were feeling our love anew,
For we brought our moments to full fruition.
Each of us possessed enough love for two,
And we yielded without any condition.

II

We exchanged rings and had our share of bliss,
Though our love needed no rings to persist.
As we shared our love, I realized this:
'A beloved grows lovelier when she's kissed.'

When I know that I am already blessed;
I set free the bird of love from her cage,
And allowed her to choose her tree to nest,
In there, to sing now sweetly, then in rage.

III

The seeds of love at first sight find a site
In the hearts of lovers to keep alive.
They can't sprout as soon as they see the light
Without waiting for the spring to arrive.

What's the limits for love's intensity?
At what degree I will begin to burn?
When I burn, shall an extra love cure me?
When I'm nearer love, why do I still yearn?

What's known about love's true identity?
Shall she grow old and her just due is dealt?
Is she an enrapturing energy,
Which can't be heard or seen but only felt?

IV

When glaring full moon poured down its cool light,
We cupped our hands and filled them full to shower
Each other to quell the heat of the night;
Then we celebrated our finest hour.

In the game of love nothing works for sure,
I may leave her behind by being swift;
Or being slow, I may chance upon her,
Or she'll come as an unexpected gift.

Love will not always take the easy street.
She may choose to wander through the desert;
May not find the path to the bridal suite,
Yet she knows who's a lover, who's a flirt.

We thought that love always climbs to the crest
To reign up there, and never to decline.
But then a slight rift became manifest
Between us, which we could not realign.

V

Finally we split apart and went our way.
The days that we spent together became
Our halcyon days; and love had her say,
"Be aware! I'm the lovers' smokeless flame."

I drank the dregs not to leave residue,
Still my burning desires I could not slake.
I learned my biggest lesson through you;
There can be no parting without heartache.

I have forgotten the major events,
But the little things I remember well:
Shared first meal, exchanged carefree compliments,
A red rose or a yellow asphodel.

Yesterday's endearments have now grown stale,
Still, loving memories stay just the same.
As the same song's sung by the nightingale;
As if it's my mantra, I sing your name.

Our common sense told us to give-and-take,
But one way is the journey of a lover,
Once one is lost, the whole trip is at stake;
Naught could be left to salvage or recover.

VI

We would know when a love affair began
Yet we could not know when it'll run its course.
Unpredictable is the love's life span,
For she draws her vigor from a veiled source.

I'm not alone. I don't just reminisce,
I'm in touch with you through telepathy.
If you wish you may, but I can't dismiss
Our shared love since it is a part of me.

VII

Young lovers' fragrant roses never fade,
Still their noses favor each other's scent.
At each dawn, as nightingales serenade,
They sip love's elixir with merriment.

It is pitiful that lovers grow wise;
They'd no longer feel but judge and justify.
Their wisdom dims the twinkle in their eyes,
And their shared dreams grow obscure by-and-by.

Who knows what's distilled? What's the residue?
Since our feelings are fused I still feel you.

Harmony on Earth?

Brent Cliff Swallow and Fern Barn Swallow fell
In love and friends gave aid and admonition;
Plus, the lovebirds were told, "No one can quell
The fumes of the keepers of the tradition."

Bride and groom wished to use the tongue of birds
In temple to seal their vows with a tweet.
They were cut short and told, "Repeat the words
After the keepers of the Holy Writ."

The flock went south in line with approved plan.
The young pair chose a new route with less drag;
They were stopped in flight and told, "No one can
Change the rules of the keepers of the flag."

How much accord can we expect from souls
Living on a world with opposing poles?

Is it Possible to Possess?

Be my guest! Take what your heart might desire.
Acquire much wealth by being a worldling,
And hoard them to build a worthless empire.
Me? I know this: I can possess Nothing.

I barely borrowed this handful of dust
Which can be scattered with a sudden gust.

Trust

One day, Jane slipped off her engagement ring,
And waved bye-bye. When she was at the door,
I asked, "What's wrong?" She just shrugged, "Not a thing,
Except that, I don't love you any more."

The next day, my boss gave me the pink slip.
I said, "Where have I gone wrong? Tell me Bob."
He grinned, "We are proud of your workmanship,
But you're overqualified for this job."

I said to myself, "Zeke, no need to fret,
Just be thankful for not hitting the dust,
You'll bounce back, keep trying and don't forget
There are plenty of people you can trust."

I trusted to my parents in my teens
For I'd been duped while acquiring their genes.

Parallel Paths

"Without the hopes of heaven and horrors of hell,"
Priests say, "Folk won't follow the path; they'll go astray."
Still men will do a good deed and wish others well.

Free thinkers will have thoughts which conformists can't quell;
And they follow their nous to the end and won't sway
With the hopes of heaven and the horrors of hell.

Against the customs of the flock, some will rebel,
And blaze a new path for all to use and as they
Journey, they'll do a good deed and wish others well.

Some shall be at peace when they hear the final knell
Knowing that, they've already made their final pay
Without the hopes of heaven and horrors of hell.

Who's the Isaiah? And who's the Immanuel?
Some may never know but they go out of their way
Just to do a good deed and to wish others well.

When will the Judgment Day take place? Who can foretell?
Rather than wait, some seek the Enlightenment Day
Without the hopes of heaven and horrors of hell,
People will do a good deed and wish others well.

Power of the Powerless

Let the rotten rafters of this house creak,
Let its pile of brittle bricks crumble down
Or cave in. Who cares? I'm resolved to eke
Out a little income in a boom town.

Still this dismal place lures me for the bones
Of my ancestors lie under its stones.

I Demand Justice

Lawyers twist the truth to keep the rumors afloat.
It's said, "Craftiness is the sole tool of defense."
I must seek justice through my slashed and silenced throat.

To gain the jurors' sympathy, they fawn and dote
Over them while befogging their intelligence.
Lawyers twist the truth to keep the rumors afloat.

A jury's verdict isn't final. It won't denote,
"He's not guilty. I'm not a prey of violence."
I demand justice through my slashed and silenced throat.

By the Law, the judge is neutral, and can't promote
Justice, while the shysters are swayed by affluence.
Lawyers twist the truth to keep the rumors afloat.

Pass your judgment but don't be gagged by no one's vote.
I must yield my corpse to save my soul's innocence,
And must seek justice through my slashed and silenced throat.

Jurors ablated the facts then found a scapegoat
And a shred of doubt in the depths of evidence.
Lawyers twist the truth to keep rumors afloat.
I demand justice through my slashed and silenced throat.

Wonderful World

Game if fixed! No one wins the final race.
At forty, we all pass the midway line.
And yet, this world is a wonderful place.

Some people take the short cut to outpace
While others wind, yet all paths intertwine;
Game is fixed! No one wins the final race.

One has the right to have one's dreams and chase
After dreams; faced with fate, one must resign.
And yet, this world is a wonderful place.

One may be on the alert, plan and brace
Himself for unknown. One may be supine.
Game is fixed! No one wins the final race.

Once you had a playfulness in your face.
Now the flesh is weak while head is leonine,
And yet, this world is a wonderful place.

Man's worth is measured only by his space
Which may be taken without any sign.
Game is fixed! No one wins the final race
And yet, this world is a wonderful place.

One Can Cast a Tall Shadow

To leave the oppressive heat of August behind,
I climbed high and higher to catch the mountain breeze.
At noon short shadows of pine trees were intertwined.
At sunset my shadow grew as tall as pine trees.

Yesteryears' profound ideas may become shallow.
At the right time and right place, one casts a tall shadow.

Ancient Play Ground

Amphitheater is empty; no one's around
For audience and actors are at intermission.
Listen! In this hollow place silence will resound.

Look! The lower seats are buried under a mound,
Still the upper seats are maintaining their position.
Amphitheater is empty; no one's around.

The walls are cracked by the pull of the shifting ground,
And the change is an inevitable condition.
Listen! In this hollow place silence will resound.

Once they performed tragedies and young girls drowned
Themselves in tears while rulers sat stiff in suspicion.
Now the stage is empty; there is no one around.

Once they played comedies and fools were crowned,
And the tyrants were taunted without inhibition.
Listen! In this hollow place silence will resound.

Men's quests are mostly shallow but seldom profound,
And rarely their ventures can be brought to fruition.
Amphitheater is empty; no one's around.
Listen! In this hollow place silence will resound.

The True Color of Any Flag

Every nation may progress and prosper, none may lag;
Each may feel proud under their distinctively different tag.
Since each nation's flag was conceived and sustained by blood,
The color of blood is the true color of any flag.

Living Fibers Fuse and Furcate

That life providing power which indwells
In a seed tries to channel itself out.
When hugged by the rain-soaked earth, the seed swells
And bursts open to offer a sound sprout.

Tender twigs of sassy saplings shoot next
To each other; being stirred with each hiss
Of the breeze, their flexible joints are flexed
To give a chance for willing leaves to kiss.

In order to broaden their breathing space,
Firm limbs of the tall trees won't overlap;
Yet to shield the frail limbs, fit ones will brace
Against the gales for they share the same sap.

A loving leaf loves his sweetheart now for
He can do nil when the autumn winds roar.

Choices

Only the naïve new breed
Resort to downers or speed;
While sophisticated people
Have been getting high on greed.

The Missing Elements

The seed refused to mix with soil or sand
To live according to her own design.
Then a gust whirled her past the fertile land.
She never grew to be a columbine.

Carrot-headed clay was neither sloven
Nor timid but he, lacking grit to burn,
Would not venture near the potter's oven.
He never baked to be a polished urn.

At the square, I bought amphorae to store
Spirits; most were fit to fill and decant,
Some leaked and a few were not fit to pour
Into, nor out, for their necks were bored scant.

No fire will start by striking steel to flint,
Unless a spark can kiss the lips of lint.

Last Trail

Harvest is almost finished and over,
I am now baling my last bale.
Pasture is empty; as an old drover
I am trailing on my last trail.

Isolated Truth

We'd prefer to form our thoughts under the impact
Of facts, however, we can't disregard the hints.
The truth, detached from sensitivity and tact
May weigh the same, though losses it's force to convince.

A dissenter can defend himself with a mere
Unexpressive snicker. Who could refute a sneer?

One Within One

I

I dived deep into the depths of
Love and rose to the state
Of bliss; then I drowned while swimming
Near the shallows of hate.

II

Pieces of the quilt of life may
Come as blue, white and red.
They stay as one, not by their color
But with the strength of their thread.

III

It takes soft words to sooth the soul.
Once a sharp word would slip
Through one's lips; it'll surely find an
Innocent heart to nip.

IV

I was crushed while facing the crowd
Because, I lost the race.
Yet among friends and neighbors, I
Did not cover my face.

V

Kids breathe life into the streets and
Vacant lots as they roam,
And turn the neighborhood into
An extension of home.

VI

My heart felt not caged in my chest,
Instead felt free to fly.
Then grew leaden as the vexed friends
And neighbors passed me by.

VII

I packed my lot with good fortunes,
Still it's empty by half.
I laugh when my friends laugh; if not,
I won't have much to laugh.

VIII

I celebrate them all: Christmas,
Ramazan and or Labor Day.
I would like to meet and cheer
My neighbor at the midway.

An Extra Touch of Smile

My Master has billions of figures in His file.
He draws them similar with a distinctive style.
He provides His uncompromising care to each,
And highlights a few with an extra touch of smile.

Daily Chores, Bygone Days and Dim Memories

For Old Man life stirring spring comes with chores.
Shortly after silencing the snow blower,
He noticed freeze dried leaves of sycamores,
Soon he must rake them to run the lawn mower.

Over the years weeping willow grew tall;
Some brittle limbs broke with the weight of snow.
Without hindrance he gathered twigs to haul;
Old Dog was dozing on the patio.

Cold winds of winter almost killed the plum;
Some suckers might grow stout to save the tree.
To make sure, he grafted a few shoots; some
Of them might take, he'll have to wait and see.

It's his birthday according to file card;
Lone! He'll feign having a ball in the yard.

Is Present Enough by Itself?

When they say, "Past is buried, future is unborn,
Live for the day." It is difficult to object.
What's the meaning of present if it were forlorn
Without a bright future and a past to reflect?

It Is Always Open

As always people begin as aquatic
Beings, and the sea is detectable
In the electrolytes of their plasmatic
Fraction; for life sea is the vehicle.

With a thousand rivers' might, ocean streams pull
And carry them all, as they churn and twist.
Yet men turn home, their sails bellying full,
For favorable winds pierce through the mist.

Enlightenment of man does not consist
Of knowing facts; the way is not exposed
Nor concealed from the man. Where roads desist,
There trails take over, and gates are not closed.

Since, "It's Open! Come In!" signs I ignore,
I should not plead, "My Lord! Open Your Door!"

Fate of Favoritism

Pond harbors, hosts and nurtures all;
   Whether they swim or crawl,
      Or fly in peace
        Like geese.
         *

       When you're
      Charmed by amour,
   And scatter corn for snow-
White chick, you'll tempt the raiding crow.

Never Learn to Unlearn

They told me, "Never bend the golden rule,
Choose and refine your words and give them straight;
Learn! Yet never learn to unlearn in school!"

Since men give and take from the same gene pool,
They have to hate themselves to learn to hate.
They told me, "Never bend the golden rule."

A fool can reach the level of tomfool.
You can give knowledge but can't educate.
Learn! Yet never learn to unlearn in school.

Man stops for a while at church, mosque or shul,
Then must keep moving for journey can't wait.
They told me, "Never bend the golden rule."

Weave the fabric of life with thread of spool.
Don't jump forward before you calculate.
Learn! Yet never learn to unlearn in school.

Touch gently, for scale is a sacred tool.
Resist temptation; it's the Devil's bait.
They told me, "Never bend the golden rule."
Learn! Yet never learn to unlearn in school.

Soil is Waiting

Soil is waiting
To be bountiful. Evermore,
Soil is waiting
To reveal its fascinating
Yet well hidden treasures of yore.
As a true friend, under my floor,
Soil is waiting.

The Gourd and the Poplar

Creepy Gourd disliked crawling on the dirt.
Though, he was too limp to stand on his own.
The Poplar advised, "Take hold of my skirt
Now and you can stand erect when you're grown."

The Poplar served as a spine for the Gourd,
And Gourd clung with vigor to Poplar's stocky
Body and grew fast on free room and board;
Reaching the top, he bore fruit then got cocky.

The Gourd told Poplar, "You're dense and dull, heck,
In a single warm season, I grew tall
Enough to hang my nuts around your neck."
Poplar, "After the summer comes the fall."

Killing frost fell on them. Poplar stood straight,
While Gourd hit the dirt under its own weight.

The Old Mountain Goat and The Kid

Old Goat said, "Kid! There is no such thing as free oat.
I'm free and alive, though I took it on the chin.
Goatherd will fatten you before cutting your throat."

On high country grass, Kid grew fast and learned to float
Down from the cliffs and was heading toward the bin.
Then Old Goat warned, "There is no such thing as free oat."

As Kid grew firm jagged rocks started to denote
Freedom and he did not mind the scars on his shin
For none was feeding him before cutting his throat.

After sprouting beard and horns, Kid liked to misquote
Old Goat for he was still a kid beneath his skin.
He would say, "One can eat and get fat on wild oat."

There's no such thing as one billy goat and one vote.
When your goatherd strokes your back, you better be thin,
Thus he'll feed you longer before cutting your throat.

When goatherd is lost on a goat trail, he'll promote
You to save his own skin, and still won't let you win.
Old Goat said, "Kid! There is no such thing as free oat,
Goatherd will fatten you before cutting your throat."

Treat my Liver Tenderly

While other members of the colony
Slept and recovered in the dead of night,
Heart was pumping at full capacity
And Liver was toiling with all her might.

Liver said, "We've known each other since birth.
I synthesize things and store glycogen,
That is the why, I am gross around my girth,
So they take me for a comedian.

"You sweet Heart! You get the love and affection,
For you've an inborn rhythm and can dance.
They squander lavishly for your protection;
If you'd have pain, they call the ambulance.

"You circulate the blood which deserves
Some credit, however, when you thump
Out a lubb-dupp tune, it gets on my nerves.
Should I expect more from a living pump?

"We have lots of bums here. Who needs the Spleen?
She's merely a scavenger with a thirst
For dead blood cells. She gets cross and mean
And threatens our lives if she were to burst.

"Why do we have to feed the brain? We never
Use it; we might learn some but we can't retain.
Who'd miss the legs? If a bomb were to severe
Them, we'd've prosthesis which won't tire or pain.

46

"If I don't conjugate and clear the bile,
Everybody would turn yellowish-green.
They'll suffer from an intense itching while
They grow too weak to harvest or to glean.

"I don't mind if people have their death wish,
Without hurting their liver through the years
With their hard booze. When I grow feverish
They try to cool me down with more light beers.

"Your role is both useful and dramatic.
When you stop working, death will claim the cell
And the soul goes heaven, while in hepatic
Coma, all organs will suffer in hell."

Heart said, "You deserve more praise than you get,
Since you perform vital tasks, I agree,
No one should be judged by her silhouette,
Yet new drugs can't cure an old injury.

"The behavior of people is bizarre.
They give lip service to their brains while they
Follow their passion. With mere fact, how are
We going to get the lovers to say?

"Treat my liver tenderly, please don't shiver.
I love you from the bottom of my liver."

Old Orchard

In this Old Orchard once lived healthy trees.
Their limbs were welded seamless to their boles.
Their blooms would lure even the bashful bees;
And could bend their branches like fishing poles.

They'd turn their pink bloom into Red Delicious,
Also last year's yield they'd try to exceed.
Even so, Orchard man would grow suspicious
For no bountiful crop would quench his greed.

High yield of each passing year took its toll.
Their joints split and cracked bark grew gloomy gray.
Larvae swarmed and bruised leaves rolled like a scroll,
For orchardman did not bother to spray.

For old trees, a few apples were their best.
I did not pick for trees deserved their rest.

Life Spells out its Intentions

I

We cannot tilt the world more than a tiny fly,
And all of us arrive here as a neophyte.
Since some people are born to lose why should they try?
Grab what's thrown at you for you don't have a birthright.

I can't compete! I don't have the prerequisite,
For my inherited gifts are inadequate.

II

When nature creates and then grinds down, that makes sense;
If it's our turn to receive, we hope for a treat.
Life comes with a sentence for which we've no defense;
Still that should not make the days of our lives less sweet.

Life spells out its intentions; no need to misread.
Each flower comes through the shattered shell of a seed.

One More Breath

One may be touched by life, yet may not be caressed,
And everyone must gamble with one's destiny.
Take one more breath for each fresh breath will feel the best.

The truth is smooth to swallow, though tough to digest,
Unless it's covered with a coat of sophistry.
One may be touched by life, yet may not be caressed.

At an opportune time, one may ride on the crest   Of a
wave, though mostly he'll be tossed on the sea.
Take one more breath for each fresh breath will feel the best..

One may wish to forget: who's the host? who's the guest?
And soon, one will be reminded who holds the key.
One may be touched by life, yet may not be caressed.

To this world, every package arrives self-addressed,
Though no one shall know the day of delivery.
Take one more breath for each fresh breath will feel the best.

We ignore the signs, even when they're manifest,
And we confab about the immortality.
One may be touched by life, yet may not be caressed.
Take one more breath for each fresh breath will feel the best.

Wisdom

I

The sea spawned and cast me on the dry land.
Though she is not settled with me, therefore
She lures me with playful waves to have and
To hold me in her depths forevermore.

II

Superficially, there is not much to fear
On the land for it won't churn, foam or spray.
Although there is no safe spot on this Sphere;
For earth already snared me as its prey.

III

I've labored in the maze of mines a mile
Below the earth, and breathed a nebula
Of dust to support my family while
Enameling my lungs with silica.

IV

I learned when to plow, when to sow the grain,
But don't know how to rule the heaven's gate
To control the right timing of the rain.
It comes either too early or too late.

V
Armed with a chain saw, I felled old trees faster
Than Paul Bunyan. They say, "Young trees will reign
Over the hills in spite of that disaster."
Surely, I'll never see that day again.

Through trials, I've learned all the wisdom I need.
"The seed turns to weed; then the weed turns to seed."

No Regret

I said, "I am saving or wasting time."
As if I can control systems and signs.
I tried though I did not attain my prime,
For I missed the secrets between the lines.

On life's high wire I played without a net,
Wire's tension was flawed; still I've no regret.

When I Say "Thank You" I Said It All

Vastness of the Cosmos boggles my mind.
There, there's no destination to arrive,
No getting ahead or falling behind.
The only marvel is being alive.

I neglected my prayers, it is true,
Then redeemed myself by saying Thank You.

Open Sores

It's prudent to take measures to be safe,
But there are no snug harbors at far shores.
Even smooth rubbing can cause chronic chafe,
Though, remedies aren't kept behind lock doors.

Our exposed sides we don't want to ignore,
Yet life lasts even with an open sore.

It's Your Fault

I

I can't find any healthful food to eat.
Who's curing produce to taste like corn silk?
Who's letting hormones dribble into meat?
Who's adding antibiotics to milk?

Since childhood you've fed me sugar and salt.
If I'm morbidly obese, it's your fault.

II

Its use in Holy Communion makes wine
Deserving to be used in moderation.
When something is rationed, people incline
To consume it beyond habituation.

You taught me to sip weak liquors of malt,
If I'm an alcoholic, it's your fault.

III

Kids with poor genes like me can be assigned
To complex courses though few can complete.
I'm the slow kid who was not left behind,
Still with global workers, I can't compete.

You set wrong ways in motion, I can't halt,
If I can't attain my goals, it's your fault.

IV

My Father came home and grabbed the remote control
After laboring a dead-end job for the buck.
He might have bemoaned about his unattained goal,
Still he'd let his affairs be governed by dumb luck.

No one cared what I'd under my cranial vault.
If my brain is not well developed, it's your fault.

V

In my youth, I was not shown the inside
Of an art museum to train my eyes;
Frivolous engagements were glorified,
And art objects were prized as merchandize.

You taught me not what's worthy to exalt;
If my value scale is wrong, it's your fault.

VI

When I was drunk and felt exposed, I fantasized
A world where I would feel safe even when spaced-out.
I assessed life once more when I was soberized;
There I found blessings but nothing to whine about.

If I build my house on a bog, not on basalt,
Because of inaccurate judgment, it's my fault.

They Live on in a Shell

People like to spin convoluted tales
To amuse themselves, and not to reveal
Their plans as they go on their private trails.
Souls wear smiles or frowns to hide how they feel.

What's hidden in men's hearts no one can tell
For each one of them live on in a shell.

I Played Without Knowing All the Rules

With hidden traps of life I came to terms,
And I steered around them with some success.
However, ultimate result affirms
That when the ways were veiled I had to guess.

Perhaps certain secrets I was not meant to learn,
Before my ashes were packed into a cold urn.

Then, Now and Always

I

We no longer classify the people as slaves
Or citizens; we now split them into elite,
Ordinary folks, and a small fraction of knaves.
We still have our bias but we are now discreet.

Now thieves function within the law and rob
Us daily by retiring on the job.

II

Fates of poor men and bats are somehow similar,
Since without help they must govern their destiny.
Surely a bat can fly better than a chukar,
And yet, bats aren't embraced by birds' society.

A poor man digs for gold but can't find a potsherd.
A bat can fly though can't grow feathers like a bird.

III

The lust to rule is stronger than of yore;
That's why 'brain washing' is still pertinent.
They say, "We love free thoughts," and soon they pour
Statements like 'tradition' as diluent.

Folks teach kids what not to say when they're young,
Then let them make use of their civil tongue.

IV

Nowadays ancient truths are vanishing.
We don't think clean air has a healing power.
As long as this planet turns around, spring
Has to come with or without a fresh flower.

To fill our guts we need fiber and fruit,
To get those, we strangle the soil en route.

V

A physician cannot practice without
Knowing the case. During Hippocrates'
Times they knew all there was to know about
The patient but not about his disease.

When medicine's goal is to cure, we score
Higher now, but do we care anymore?

VI

After having a shortage of virgins,
They quit practicing human sacrifice.
Folks can't cast the first stone; they've their own sins,
Now adulteresses live in paradise.

Nowadays it's easy to be lovebirds
For love songs are sung with four letter words.

VII

People do not repeat the same mistake.
Heretics are safe now for we don't skin
Them alive, don't burn witches at a stake,
And for blood baths don't use a guillotine.

Now we make trials of criminals fair;
Then fry them in a comfortable chair.

VIII

People stick to old ways while changing their beliefs.
Now they shy away from practicing annual
Bacchanalia, but just as aperitifs
They consume wine daily just like a bacchanal.

Now, people let their mediocrity run free
While they're bottling and corking their excellency.

IX

Greeks thought that it was love's most desirable form.
Hebrews tried to conceal it with duplicity.
They did it before and after Sodom's fire storm,
Now they're trying to clean the word of sodomy.

Now a gay couple can walk down the aisle,
For it's called, "An alternative life style."

X

Putting public perks on the auction block
Was always a relapsing social plague.
Public servants' fleecing the subdued flock
Was called 'bribery'; nil was veiled or vague.

Now with its new names bribery sounds lawful,
For gifts and speaking fees don't sound so awful.

XI

When they heard "Know thyself' none liked the thy,
But they loved the self; and tried self-control.
Folks were bewitched by self-love at first try.
Since then self sucks them in like a black hole.

With self-gratification, we're obsessed,
And can't wean ourselves from self-interest.

XII

"Stick the needle into thyself before
Sticking the knife into another soul."
Old needles were not fun for they'd no bore;
And taking dope with them was not the goal.

Now we stick the needle into our vein,
And fry our brains by the fire of cocaine.

Nature Won't Forewarn

I labored to raise rose bushes without a thorn
To give smooth shoots for nightingales to serenade.
Nature brings its changes but won't forewarn.
So doomsday shall come to pass sans my aid.

I had seeds to plant. Then seasons changed, so did I.
The change is natural, no reason to ask why.

A Child's Curiosity in a Man

I stopped and watched highway building machines with awe,
For in men's hands they build as well as they destroy.
So, when I was old enough to drink with a straw,
I wanted to know all about my Tonka toy.

Keeping some innate traits alive is nature's plan,
Thus we find a child's curiosity in a man.

Feed me False Hopes

The script of life has been written sans a finis,
So, all have to act and pay the ultimate price.
Here, I am preoccupied to seek happiness;
Hereafter, I'll find timeless bliss in paradise.

Don't tell me, "One loses while another prevails."
Cast a spell over me by telling fairy tales.

Drifting Dreams

Whether I've five or five hundred and five,
Still they are all within my element,
Provided I'm happy being alive,
For life is the sole heaven-sent present.

Since facts don't change according to my schemes,
I might as well have frameless flighty dreams.

Unshared Grief

Somehow, I left my native land behind;
In this place, I turned over a new leaf.
Supportive new friends were not hard to find;
Though, being new they could not feel my grief.

I'll get along in this land on my own,
If I can get used to moaning alone.

Fickleness of Fate

First I reviewed the Farmer's Almanac,
Then I sowed my seeds when the days were warm.
Having no more work to do, I set back.
Soon, my plants perished in a rare ice storm.

Some facts of life, we don't like to address,
Yet, freak mishaps are part of life's process.

Forever Young

You conquered my heart and started your reign,
Then let me fall behind by shifting gears.
Since your youthful face was stamped on my brain,
It had no graceful change over the years.

If I search for you in a crowded place,
I may not recognize your mature face.

Happiness Is an Illusion

One day we open our eyes, here we are,
In front of things to choose from and collage.
From a distance, bliss glitters like a star,
When we draw near, it fades like a mirage.

We are here to survive and reproduce,
But happiness harbors no useful use.

Shrouded Slyness

All living things have a hidden dimension;
For self-fulfillment they resort to guile.
Flowers ooze fragrance to draw bees' attention
To their private parts to remain fertile.

I fell for a Wild Flower by a brooklet,
Then found her name in a 'Noxious Weeds' booklet.

What Is Not Enough for Herds Is Ample for Bees and Birds

Snow is gone and deer moved to higher ground;
So, I'm not obliged to give salt and oats.
Creek is running low; no deer tracks around.
It is time to foal and shed winter coats.

In these days, creek can't quench the thirst of herds,
But it saved some seepage for bees and birds.

Evolution Must Have a Hidden Helper

Who made a fang by hollowing a tooth
To allow a snake envenom its prey?
Now there's no way to verify the truth,
For few signs stay but most of them decay.

Evolution's chance to coin fangs is nil
Unless it's skillful with a dentist's drill.

Our Feelings Judge the Length of Time

Shortest distance between two points is set,
Though journey's time would change from day to day.
I used to stroll by a swift rivulet,
Now I whiz by for the stanch of decay.

To hike the familiar trail took me extra hours,
For I zigzagged not to stomp on the wild flowers.

The End Is Fated But Not Welcome

To have a good time, no place is taboo.
I picked the Earth for it's a free resort
And hailed all cheers coming out of the blue,
For distance between life and death is short.

I've lived so long if I die now it's fair,
Yet my lungs long for one more breath of air.

No Reason to Fret

I was given advantages before I was born;
If what I received were not gifts, I can't pay back.
In this vast world, I will always be a greenhorn;
Then I'll pass through the gate with an empty back pack.

In crocuses bed, I like to be slumbering
For their bulbs bloom the earliest in every spring.

Chasing After a Goal

I've hiked when bitter cold winter wind blew,
And for me, no rimrock was a roadblock.
Here is the hole on the sole of my shoe,
And the wear of use on my alpenstock.

If I've already seen the earth from pole-to-pole,
That does not mean that I am closer to my goal.

As the World Turns, People Get Pushed Aside

I said to myself, "I won't be alone;
My ties with living things are infinite."
Then the Devil said, "Your friends can disown
And push you aside before you know it."

Lives of Countless Nows

I

Every life form starts with vigor and vim
For perplexing and veiled life forces cause
Stem cells to become a brain or a limb.
Then they grow dormant in line with their laws.

The Reaper reaps and leaves nothing to glean,
Life means merely what we think it may mean.

II

It takes one fertilized egg to divide
Into cells that perform a unique role;
As daughter cells specialize, they abide
By laws which save the soleness of the soul.

I came with the core of life packed in me,
Yet all twists of life are a mystery.

III

I'm in a womb where my cells multiply
To become a viable neonate.
I thrive on mother's milk and lullaby,
And I've the potential to procreate.

With each heartbeat I extol you, my Lord,
You fed me through an umbilical cord.

IV

I'm an infant and mostly stay abed,
Yet I possess an eager-to-learn brain.
From baby's mouth you'll hear back what you said
For my brain can't judge but it can retain.

An infant's formative brain holds no clutter,
Thus, it'll register what ever you utter.

V

In my early childhood I learned to speak
Which is a momentous accomplishment.
I still continue to play hide-and-seek,
For my growth all efforts are pertinent.

My destination may be far away,
With baby steps, I'll reach there as I play.

VI

In my preteens I am given the facts
Of life which sound new though they are age-old;
Drama of life is played in many acts,
For its real meaning is manifold.

In my preteens, I mostly make good sense,
Yet my impatience shows my impudence.

VII

At puberty a renewal takes place.
I behold the world under a pink light.
A girl flaunts a flirty smile on her face.
I chase her with a blend of grit and fright.

Just at right seasons beasts get to be wooed
While men are always in a mating mood.

VIII

In my teens I burn up my baby fat,
And develop spidery arms and legs.
I embrace life without a caveat.
I am young to bear, though I've sperm or eggs.

A teenager's balance is imprecise;
Like the poise of calves romping on pond ice.

IX

In my late teens my growth is incomplete,
And my brain expands with each new neuron.
I'm being remolded with each heart beat,
Plus spiritual growth goes on and on.

I can't control my emotions for sure;
My prefrontal cortex is immature.

X

In my twenties I am in a transition.
High school and parents' house are left behind,
But my new quest has not come to fruition.
Still a sketch of success stamped in my mind.

In my twenties I see my destination,
Still I must move ahead with dedication.

XI

In my thirties I've a full membership
In society and I'm satisfied;
I'm a new member but I've a good grip
On my credentials and they're bona fide.

In my thirties I'm like a full-grown tree.
I've a nesting site for a chickadee.

XII

In my forties I'm a self-assured man.
I push ahead to realize my goals
Without wavering I follow my plan,
Still, I would esteem the support of souls.

In my forties I've enough energy
And grits to govern my own destiny.

XIII

In my fifties I have reached the apex
Of my professional and earning range.
Bonding with my family grow complex;
Our ties turn loose but their strength does not change.

In my fifties I feel firm and secure,
I've smarts to change my plight or to endure.

XIV

In my sixties lifestyle changes take place,
I must give to receive; can't pick and choose.
Retirement and less income I must face;
Still my expertise I can put to use.

In my sixties I attempt to hold on
To my gifts but must ditch what is far gone.

XV

In my early seventies I'm retired;
I strive to dwell at this side of the portal,
And like to score before my time's expired,
For it's rumored that no one is immortal.

I've no time to waste in indecision;
I'll publish my book sans one more revision.

XVI

In my eighties I've enough time to pull
Loose ends together and let them be furled.
I don't find staying past my time mirthful,
Yet, I hate to go near the Netherworld.

In my eighties I'm not completely spent,
Though, on this Sphere nothing is permanent.

XVII

In my nineties I'm not old but old-old,
I don't know why I'm living anymore.
Am I waiting for my fate to unfold?
For there's a special surprise for each soul.

Even in my nineties life bugs and baits,
Soon I'll tell you about the Pearly Gates.

XVIII

In my hundreds I must keep company
With myself and like it for I've no choice.
And must ignore my ebbing energy;
Still each breath is an event to rejoice.

Now I have no living lover or friend,
Though Mother Earth shall hug me to the end.

XIX

One may live to be one hundred and twenty-five,
Although, he'll be a shadow of his youthful days,
And there are many levels of being alive.
I don't say always but the death happens always.

One may be living a long life and may look spry,
Still hundred years fly off just like a blink of an eye

XX

To this world I'm given a free entrance,
Though I did not know what it meant to me.
But I should have realized at first glance
That life itself has no mortality.

What might fall on this world is past my guess.
I'm living in the state of thankfulness.

XXI

With some luck I came into existence.
I'm not asked to appraise anything's worth.
Yet I'd say wise lovers keep some distance,
Still I am getting closer to the Earth.

Before I go, I won't compose a sequence,
I'd rather leave behind a stark silence.

XXII

In order to predict how my life would turn out,
I used up the realm of logic with whys and hows.
Then I fostered false hopes but soon started to doubt,
For I don't have one life but lives of countless nows.

When I was young, "Your future is bright," I was told,
Though, no one said, "Don't borrow worries when you're old."

XXIII

I indulged in life when I had the chance,
Still I'd hate to come back and live once more,
For I'll be lost in a new life's expanse,
Since nothing shall be like I had before.

An individual life is created
Under the terms that can't be duplicated.

I Outgrew my Worldly Berth

Life won't grow joyous by adding more years.
I had an "Eternal Moment" in my youth,
And joined with The One and conquered my fears
Of death before I grew long in the tooth.

I learned my lessons in the school of earth,
Then left, for I outgrew my worldly berth.

Promise

"Worldly existence is fleeting," they say,
"Besides, time is not under your purview.
"To the natural laws you must obey.
"Still eternal life is promised to you."

If my first stop is a Necropolis,
Then I can't enjoy the heavenly bliss.

After All These Years

I make firm plans, and then life interferes;
With each sunset the thread of life wears thin,
Yet my love stays young after all these years.

I may be fit but the bout may be fierce,
And my best may not be enough to win.
I make firm plans, and then life interferes.

Into the marvels of life I can't pierce,
For the simplest change shrouds its origin.
Yet my love stays young after all these years.

I can't rinse the trace of failed love with tears,
And as I watch the schemes of life I grin.
I make firm plans, and then life interferes.

When I'm weary of my plight I change gears,
And I slow down to prevent a tailspin,
Thus my love stays young after all these years.

When my lover whispers I am all ears,
And prep my heart for her love to roll in.
I make firm plans, and then life interferes,
Yet my love stays young after all these years.

Noninterference

I

Their well-accepted ideas grow mean
When they try to curb our dissenting thoughts.
Ideas thrive when we don't intervene.
In fact, they outlived eons of onslaughts.

On this earth, we could create sterile zones
By repopulating them with our clones

II

We use new ways to probe the mustard seeds,
But faiths use ways to keep their ascendance,
And new vocabularies of old creeds
Contain no words that might mean tolerance.

Our craving for the brain's hints is unsated,
Although intelligence is overrated.

Christmas

I celebrate the birthday of the Man
Who dared to command, "Turn the other cheek,"
And offered his body as a corban;
Thus, clearing the love's path for mighty and meek.

Forces Are in a State of Flux

I'm blessed for I can't reshape water in my hand,
To create life, it must stay shapeless and must flow.
Calamities happen, whether I understand,
For Forces are fickle as they'd been long ago.

After a soft shower, leaves turn a deeper green,
And after shedding cleansing tears souls grow serene.

Meals Eaten Alone Bloat the Guts But Can't Soothe the Soul

We backed up each other to kill the prey,
And carried it to our communal cave.
Medicine man fed the young and the gray,
Regardless if the soul were base or brave.

Any food nourishes the body of a beast,
Though, meager meals shared with friends turn into a feast.

Happiness

Since ancient times wise men tried to define,
What happiness is and how to get it?
Nobody came up with a sound guideline,
Though a full life is a prerequisite.

I let old prescriptions rest on the shelf;
I'm happy when I'm at peace with myself.

Hafiz of Develi

I. Birthday of Hafiz

Hafiz of Develi was adopted
By many trade unions as a brother,
And well respected by everybody.

To celebrate his one hundredth birthday
People mobilized from every district
Of the city and they assembled at
The Coliseum by the Elbiz Spring.

II. Seven Springs of Develi

Develi is spread around the Seven Springs.
The Elbiz Spring is centrally located,
And it has the highest flow rate per second.

Its year-round even flow is regulated
By the ample Mt. Erciyes Aquifer.
In return, Elbiz Spring supplies vital
Water to houses, orchards and gardens.

Spring-fed Elbiz Pond is clear and tranquil,
Though it's too deep for kids to swim safely.
Downstream provides shallows for them to splash.

The park around the Pond is covered with
Jointed ayrik grass and shaded with sycamores.
Since this Spring was the reason why the central
City was established at its present location,
Folks keep observing their main events there.

When the people got their fill from the feast,
And finished dancing they gathered together
In the Coliseum to extol Hafiz.

Everyone, young or old, wore a broad smile
As if resolved to celebrate the day
Regardless of sunshine or thunderstorm.

III. A Self Appointed Historian

Koca Kamil stood first to spin tall tales.
He is a self-appointed historian
Who does not mind mixing facts with fancy.

"Hafiz was born in eighteen-eighty-two.
He was a robust baby boy though blind.
Since his early childhood, people called him
'Hafiz' which is not a name but a title.
He earned that title by memorizing
The entire Koran at the age of six.

"During his teens people recognized his
Moral steadfastness so they adopted
Him as one of their accomplished citizens.
Folks forgot his first and last name but fondly
They renamed him 'Hafiz of Develi.'

"Eighteen eighties were lean years for a blind
Child for those years were also declining
Years for the Mighty Ottoman Empire.

"At the remote provinces no schools were
Nearby for the teaching of blind children;
And the schools at Istanbul were beyond
The reach of young Hafiz's family.

"In those days, blind boys were raised to become
A hafiz to function as a muezzin,
To call the faithful people to the mosque,
And to do minor functions for a pittance,
Or to perform certain religious rites
At private residences to receive pay
Which was not much more than receiving alms.

"Another option for a blind boy was
To become a musician to perform

At local festivities and weddings.
Blind male musicians were preferred by ladies,
For they did not have to cover themselves,
In front of the ogling eyes of a man,
So they could dance uninhibitedly."

When I was a boy, famous musicians were
Blind Onnik and his wife Dudu Oksana.
I overheard some old ladies gossiping.
'Onnik is not blind. It is just an act.
When a young beautiful girl starts to dance,
He immediately plays lively tunes'

"Hafiz did advanced studies and became
An ordained imam. He worked as such for
Several years at the Aloglu Mosque.

"Even when he was a child he must have
Known that life begins with self-reliance.
He wanted to have something tangible
To sell in order to receive payment.
He taught himself carpentry, masonry,
Locksmithing and became an inventor.
Well qualified people will testify
About his tremendous accomplishments.

"Develi's roots go deep into the past.
Its fortress may be from the Hittite times.
Though no one can be sure of that until
A scientific archeological
Study is done; even then it won't be
Conclusive for over the years it had
Been often stripped by the fortune seekers.

"From the Seljuk Turks Develi acquired
Historical buildings which are well kept.

"Develi harbored multiple cultures
Preferred by Armenians, Greeks and Turks.

"Before the collapse of the Turkish Empire
Non-Turkish young men were more fortunate
Than young Turks, for non-Turks were not drafted,
While young Turks were expected to prop up
Their crumbling Empire with years of service.

"If young Turks were lucky to return home,
They had to build their lives from the beginning,
While their non-Turkish comrades had finished
Their education, established their business,
Married and had several healthy children.

"Before the beginning of World War I,
Turks were already fighting in the Balkans.
When the Big War was over, the long-lived
Turkish Empire was dead; most of the Mother
Land was occupied by the Western Powers.

"Social order was completely disrupted.
Mistrustfulness and paranoia
Afflicted every ethnic group which fostered
An uncertain atmosphere of chaos.
So I will not judge now what happened then.

"One thing was clear; nobody was afraid
Of death for it was a welcome outcome.
They were reciting Seyrani's quatrain.

"'Since I'm unemployed no one can fire me.
I'm just a sacrificial billy goat.
Don't delay my journey with false promises.
I'm ready, when you decide; cut my throat.'"

"When the freedom war was won by the Turks,
They formed The Republic of Turkiye
In the blessed year of nineteen twenty-three.
Then Greeks and Turks exchanged their ethnic people.

"I don't know if the Greeks of Develi
Missed their stately homes adorned with statues.
But I'm sure the Greek poet, Son of Nikos,
Missed the streams with grebolu bushes growing
Alongside to provide personal pockets
Of small hiding places for him to read
His bible in Turkish and write his poems.

"'We're safe for no thugs are at large
To harm me or my spouse.
To hone their skills, thieves and crooks are
Gathered in the courthouse.'"

IV. Childhood Memories

While Koca Kamil was kept talking my
Mind blocked what he was saying and shifted
To my childhood memories which were tied
Directly or indirectly with Hafiz.

His shop was located at the Old Town,
While most of the stores and workshops were moved
To popular districts at the New Town.

We, the neighborhood kids, were attracted
To the Old Town because an indoor swimming
Pool was located there and we were welcome.

On the way to the pool we'd pass other
Attractions that peaked our curiosity.
There was a complex of old derelict buildings
Which were enclosed by a high tuff stonewall
Which was unevenly covered with weeds
Growing in the cracks of the crumbling stones.

Adults referred to that place as 'The Saray'
Because the administration buildings
Of the Ottoman Empire were based there.

The North Portal had been built with huge granite
Blocks which were adorned with Seljuk designs.
The portal's double doors were overlaid
With hammered copper sheets and were fastened
With bronze hobnails in a way to form puzzling
Adornments though just the star and crescent
Could be seen clearly from every angle.
They used to use these doors for wagon traffic.

At the middle of the big double doors
There was a second set of smaller doors
Which were used for pedestrian traffic.

The bigger outer doors were out of order,
And at that time their only useful function
Was to support the smaller central ones.

I feared when I passed through the central doors ,
That an imaginary uniformed
Ottoman doorkeeper would stop and to question
Me as to what office I'd business in.
Also, I had to be sure that there were
No adults to interfere, then it was
A good time to swing on the inner doors.

Most of the buildings were in utter ruin.
One had the feeling that most of the people
Died of a plague and not enough caring
People were left behind to bury them.

Big old trees were not pruned for a long time.
Thus, dead branches were mingling with green ones.
They reminded me of a frail old beggar
Who needed a clean shave and a hair cut.

In the flower beds no cultivated
Flowers or import roses could be seen.
But wild flowers and roses were flourishing
In defiance of disaster or drought.

Lawn grade grass was desiccated and dead,
Yet jointed ayrik grass was boldly thriving.
Ayrik won't grow too high above the ground,
But lets its roots go deep into topsoil.

As its stems trail on the ground, new roots grow
From each node to become a daughter plant.
As it's in a healthy society,
Each plant has its roots to survive freely,
Yet it's interconnected with its kind.

Among the ruined piles, at the northwest
Of the complex, one building was surviving
And it was functioning as a Post Office.

We were familiar with the post master.
He was the father of one of our playmates,
And a highly respected herbalist.
We all tasted his hollyhock flower
Tea every time we had cold or coughing.
Amazedly, we took it willingly
For he sweetened his tea with highland honey.

At the south side of the Saray, both the wall
And the portal were completely ruined.

V. Old Town Square

Four blocks to the south and one block to the east
Of the ruined Saray Gate, the Old Town Square
And the old Market Place was located;
There, a few run-down stores were being used.
One of those was the workshop of Hafiz.
Another building was blacksmith Haydar's
Workshop which we'd occasionally visit.

VI. Indoor Saray Swimming Pool

The indoor swimming pool was located
On the northwest side of the Town Square.
Its water was fed by the Saray Spring,
Which sprang into the pool, circulated,
Then cascaded into the Sandy Creek.

Spring's flow rate and temperature did not
Change by the seasons, though it felt cool during
The summer and warm during the winter.

There was no need to adjust the flow rate
Or the temperature of the pool's water.
Everything was done by the aquifer.

The pool was constructed with blocks of polished
Tuff stones which were laid so close to each other
That no drop of water could seep out even
If there was no mortar between the stones.

The pool was covered with a massive dome.
The portholes of the dome were located
In such a way that during the daytime
Sun rays would dance over the pool, then
Reflect over the mosaics of the dome.
It would give an illusion that designs,
Made of mosaics, were constantly changing.

No one owned the pool; no one charged a fee
To swim there; no one cared to maintain it.
One good thing, it needed no maintenance.
There was nothing to burn, nothing to rust.
Its thick walls, graceful columns and well balanced
Dome already passed the test of earthquakes.

Even when we were kids, we were curious
As to who built such an elaborate
Building over a tranquil rivulet.
Simply no one could give a truthful answer,
Still today I've no historical truth.

Saray Spring has no special qualities
To distinguish itself from other springs.
It has neither a high mineral content,
Nor is it a hot spring to qualify
As a spa to attract health conscious people
To justify a monumental building.

Its name suggests that it might have been a part
Of a royal complex, yet I would like
To think it was built by a jealous
Sovereign for his lover in order
To block the eyesight of all other men.
Thus, no living man's gaze could possibly
Penetrate into her private domain,
And surreptitiously be able to
Steal a kiss from her voluptuous lips.

VII. The Workshop of Hafiz

When we'd exhaust ourselves at the pool,
We'd stop and rest at the workshop of Hafiz.

In our eyes he was a well kept old man,
For his brown hair was graying at temples.
His skin had a glow which was said to be
Due to reflection of the light of prayers.
While talking, he always had a warm smile,
Wide enough to exhibit his white teeth.

Since he was an imam and a craftsman,
At the mosque he wore clothes like an imam,
And at his workshop as an artisan
By wearing loose pants, short sleeved shirts and vests
Which exposed his strong sinewy biceps.

His shop was a long and windowless building.
Its entire front consisted of a wide
Entrance door and heavy wooden shutters.
Bottom segment of the shutters functioned
As a broad plank for us kids to perch on.

During the daytime, sunlight could not light
The back of the shop which did not matter
For Hafiz did not need light to work any
Moment during a twenty-four hour day.

He had no shingle and/or street number
For most of his customers were not blind,
So they could find his place at the work hours.

His door consisted of an upper half
Which was kept open and a lower half
Which was kept closed and used as a counter.

We must not have been the first generation
Of kids who paid visits to Hafiz's
Workshop for we had a list of guidelines
As to how to act while visiting his shop:
Each time we entered his workshop, we were
To greet him one at a time, so that in
His mind, he could envision all of us
As one-of-a kind individuals,
Who have their personal identities.

We were not to rearrange his instruments
Or to tidy anything on his workbench,
Even if they looked to us disarranged.
We were to be absolutely quiet when
He was doing business with his customers.

We were warned, if we did not comply with
The rules, we had to take the consequences;
For Hafiz was not a helpless blind man.
On the contrary, he was a dead shot.
If he wanted to, he could hit anyone
Between the eyes with one of his big keys.

Though even when we grew restless and impish,
He did not demonstrate his marksmanship.
He said, "Young men, your mothers might be looking
For you and it's my time to take a nap."
He'd shut his shutters and go back to work.

I do not remember why we started
To visit with Hafiz in the first place
And even today I don't have an answer.

In the presence of Hafiz we were not
Conscious of our external appearances.
He could not see us to tease us with nicknames:
"Skinny Salim, Fat Ferit and Short Sakir."

He recognized us through our words and thoughts.
He knew our words were coming through young mouths.
He did not expect us to grow too soon.
More than anything else he did not preach.
At work he behaved like an artisan.

The reason for us being charmed with Hafiz,
Must have been a subconscious assurance
That to be blind did not mean to be helpless.
If we were to be blinded, it would not
Be an unsurmountable handicap
For we'd lead happy and productive lives.

From the spool of life, people are dispensed
More or less equal lengths of thread of life.
The spool of life is not under our control:
So, we cannot obtain more thread from it.
And we may not get to use what's allotted.
It's most viable when it's close to its source.
But gets weaker toward the end of it.
It's not fair but some get a tangled mass.
Thus they won't know where it begins or ends.

Hafiz must have delighted in our visits.
Even he must have lured us with his charm
Since for him we symbolized the beginning.
Thus vigorous part of the spool of life.

VIII. Early Days of the Republic of Turkiye

According to the doctrines of the early
Days of the Republic of Turkiye,
Hafiz was not an ideal role model
For the youth, since he was an Ottoman
Era person which made him a loser.

As he was also an accomplished cleric,
He was considered to be too opposed
To accepting new technological
Advancement which caused Turks' falling behind
In comparison to the Europeans.

IX. Blacksmith Haydar

At times we had tried to visit other places.
We were welcome at blacksmith Haydar's shop
Which was located nearby to Hafiz's.
It had a quite different atmosphere.
For his workshop had windows all around.
Thus it was airy and bright with sunshine.

Haydar was a young man with bulging muscles
Which we hoped to possess when we grew up.
Since he was exposed to soot, his eyes were
Lined as if he were wearing mascara.

He had background music which was set high
Enough to override the hammering
And bellowing sound of the blacksmith shop.

He analyzed the results of the soccer
Matches that took place between major teams
Which was an engaging topic for us.

He'd put his glowing iron on his anvil
And scatter shooting stars as he hammered.

Most of his visitors were idle chaps
From the fringes of the society.

After experiencing different
Places we'd return to Hafiz's shop.

X. The Priest Pool And Sergeant Barracuda

We even had a good alternative
For the Saray Pool. It was located
On the Priest Spring which was the northernmost
Tributary of the Seven Sources.
This Spring gushed through a cave at the bottom
Of a high cliff which was made of tuff stone.

Since Hittite times tuff stone had been valued
As a resource, for it was suitable
To build their houses, temples and bridges.

In the old times folk thought that both the cliff
And the cave were hindering the outflow.
Since they needed tuff stone, willingly
They quarried on the cliff and in the cave.
When they ended up with an Olympic
Swimming pool sized pothole around the spring,
Retesting showed no boost of the flow rate.

They stopped quarrying and decided to
Convert the pit into a swimming pool.

We could reach the pool via Fenese
Which happened to be the northernmost
District of City of Develi, unique
Both geographically and culturally.
Their resources were tuff and spring water.
They made a living by being quarry workers,
Stone polishers, stone masons and brick layers.

Local constructions kept old masons busy,
Young ones found jobs nine months of a year by
Being willing to work as migrant masons
All over Turkiye and foreign countries.

Ladies took care of fertile gardens,
Orchards and vineyards located along
The Priest Spring in the Fenese Canyon.

According to the seasons their produce
Stands would be piled with fruits and vegetables.

To reach the Priest Pool we would take the North
Main Street which was paved with polished rocks
Which formed designs; sidewalks were paved with tuff.
Both sides of the street had exclusive shops.
As we went northward workshops dominated,
And the main road gave way to winding lanes,
Then we'd know we were in the Fenese
Where we had to be careful in narrow
Lanes so we wouldn't end up in dead ends.
We'd shun the streets with loose Turkish Shepherds.

When we'd be out of the housing section,
We'd follow a pathway on the west bank
Of the Canyon which snaked down to the Pool.

When we arrived, we would be sure of two things:
The Pool and its surroundings would be clean
And a peg-legged man would be in charge.
His lay name was Sergeant Barracuda.
We did not know and did not care to know
If he owned the Pool or was a hired hand.
Without asking for it, his demeanor
Demanded obedience and respect.

He had confidence in the effectiveness
Of the buddy system, so paired the youngsters
And ordered that they look after each other.

He made sure that every newcomer child
Mastered the classical strokes; freestyle, spring
Board diving and diving into the cave.

He'd watch the swimmers and when he would see the slightest
Difficulty he'd jump in and rescue
The kid before he'd catch fear of water.

The next year, towards the end of April,
The weather was pleasantly warm and sunny.
We went to see if the Priest Pool was open.
We found that the gates were locked and the Turkish
Shepherds turned loose to guard the area
To prevent the preteens from climbing over
The fences to swim without a lifeguard.

We returned to the Saray Pool which was
Our second choice during the summer months.
Following an invigorating swim
We visited the workshop of Hafiz.

Hafiz said, "Let me guess; the Priest Pool's closed.
How do I know? Because it's a well known secret.
Barracuda is a decorated
Veteran of the Canakkale War.

"Every year in April he takes some time
Off and goes to Galipoli to pay
His respect to his fallen comrades and
To visit with other veterans who
Came from many countries and continents.
He has a place in his heart for the ANZACs.

"Before the war was started in April,
1915 , the Ottomans disrupted
The telephone lines so that the Allies
Could not establish communication.

"The Turkish units used couriers between
The Asiatic and the European
Shores of the Dardanelles. Barracuda
Was one of the couriers; there he lost
His right leg when a mine exploded in
The Dardanelles while performing his mission.

"As soon as his wounds healed he continued
To cross the channel as a courier.

"The Dardanelles has been cursed since ancient
Times because of its strategic location,
The narrow straits that separate Europe
From Asia and connect the Aegean Sea
With the Sea of Marmara and the Black Sea.

"The Greeks ruined Troy in order to pass
Through the Dardanelles without being
Disturbed and to reach their Black Sea colonies.

"To this day, the ghost of Queen Hecuba
Haunts the Dardanelles where she jumped from a
Greek ship and drowned not to be their captive.

"The main attack was launched with a fleet
Comprised of eighteen battleships with backing
Of an array of cruisers and destroyers.

"Britain and France tried to breach Canakkale's
Defenses devised by Winston Churchill.
The goal was to occupy Istanbul
And control the entire waterway from
The Aegean to the Black Sea to open
Up a safe supply channel to Russia.

"The losses in the Dardanelles prompted
The Allies to desist from attempts
To force the straits by naval power alone.
They knew that they were soundly defeated.

"They decided that ground forces were needed
At the Galipoli Peninsula.

"The British recruited from many lands:
Australia, New Zealand (The ANZACs),
India, Newfoundland, Nepal , Ireland,
And Egyptian auxiliary labor corps,
And even a Jewish Legion.

"France recruited from West Africa:
Senegal, Mali, Mauritania
Guinea, Ivory Coast, Burkina Faso,
Benin and Nigeria.

"In this war both the Allies and the Turks
Sustained unacceptable casualties.
The Allied troops presented perfect targets
To the machine guns of the Turks; out of
The first two hundred soldiers to disembark
Just twenty-one made it onto the beach.

"Every man of the Ottoman Fifty-
Seventh Infantry regiment was either
Killed in action or wounded; as a sign
Of respect, there is no Fifty-Seventh
Regiment in the modern Turkish army.

"In the end, total Turkish casualties
Were twice as high as the invading armies
For they took extraordinary risks.

"Invaders and the defenders developed
Mutual respect; they had amnesty
At Christmas and after major clashes,
So that both sides could claim their fallen men.

"Both sides grew reluctant to start big battles,
So they stretched barbed wires between the trenches.

"Uncle Davut, an old Ottoman batman,
Carried his platoon's washing and hung it
On the barbed wires to dry; when he finished,
He straightened his bent back and fixed his eyes
On the Allied trenches, and saluted.

"To celebrate the occasion, Allied
Fighters, at once, fired shots into the air.

"After that not just the batman did not
Attract fire; what's more a 'constant traffic'
Of gifts were thrown across no-man's land:
Dates and sweets from the Ottoman side and
Cans of beef and cigarettes from the Allied side.

"A friend of Uncle Davut said, 'I did not
Know that you were a suicidal man,
Or a lunatic who thought that his skin
Was touched by God, so it's turned bullet proof.
Did you forget that all those soldiers came
From different countries and they belonged
To many different cultures and races.
One thing we're sure: they have guns and they can shoot.'"

"Uncle Davut said, 'In the School of Trenches
One has to learn one's lesson or get killed.
I picked the perfect time when those soldiers
Were no longer kids with guns in their hands.
They graduated to be warriors.
Would a warrior shoot an unarmed man?'"

"The Turks were victorious both in naval
And land war because they were not fighting
For their empire but for their Motherland.

"Galipoli war was a great defensive
Victory in Ottoman history.

"No war is ever justified and just,
And no war would end in sweet victory.

"Today thirty-one independent nations
Owe part of their heritage to the Turks.

"The Garden of Eden witnessed its first murder
With the arrival of its first family
Because basic causes of war: anger,
Avariciousness, ambition, envy
Are present in people's normal psyche.

"We remember but don't learn from our past.
Knowing that war is not virtuous does
Not keep us from starting a brand-new war.
People find an excuse for war, including:
"One more war to prevent all future wars."

"The war is not a business of barbarians.
So called civilized folk can profit more from war.

"The culture of war won't go away by itself.
If I'm a child of a warring society,
Surely, I will sire a warring generation.

"To animals all people are war criminals,
Because men dominate without mutualism.
Creatures live in a state of war by nature.

"Greed, desire, ambition, dominance and power
Are normal but we have to learn to control them.

"I don't expect men to turn into angels,
But they must learn to share the resources
With beasts through a symbiotic life style.

"Peace is about living in coexistence.
Domestication of animals is not
Coexistence but total domination.

"Shackles of cast, creed, race, religion, gender
Prevent human beings coming together for
For the sake of peace and finding out that
They are not different from each other.

"To have genuine peace, we must cultivate
Culture of honesty, altruism and tolerance.

XI. Visitors of the Workshop of Hafiz

In addition to his paying customers,
Hafiz had steady visitors of varying
Mental and spiritual development.
Thus, we were exposed to different folks.

One of his regular visitors was
A powerfully built young man who had
A singular mental development.

Just like adults, we called him Abraham.
Since he was older than us, to show our
Respect, we should have added the title
Of "Agabey" meaning "Older Brother",
But we were stingy with words of kindness
When it came to addressing Abraham.

He did not have a mean bone in his body.
Nonetheless, we did not dare to tease him
Being afraid of his potential power.

He used to work at his family farm,
Mostly, by shepherding farm animals.
In his arms, he always carried a baby
Animal: a pup, a lamb or a kid,
With lovingness of a mother even
Though those babies were perfectly healthy;
They could get along well without his help.

Abraham's family lost their farm.
Thus he became permanently unemployed,
Because he had no marketable skills
To find another gainful employment.

He frequented the downtown and he loaded
And unloaded merchandise for the merchants.
He put into his pocket what they gave:
No regular wages, no bargaining power.

He carried packages for the old folks
From the bazaar without compensation,
Just to have some personal satisfaction,
Though he liked the bus terminal the best.
He loved to welcome the people returning
After many years, and feeling like strangers,
And soon they'd feel at home seeing Abraham
And witnessing that not everyone changed.

In late afternoons, he bought enough food
To feed himself, his mother and his dog
For the dinner; then emptied his pockets,
and the rest of the cash went to the beggars.

Abraham accumulated nothing,
Forgot nothing, and connected with nothing.
He rejoiced in his todays but lived a
Yesterdayless and tomorrowless life.

If he did not return home by sunset,
His mother would be out in town searching
For him from street to street and asking us
If we had seen Abraham by saying,
"I mean the young man who's short of shrewdness."

Our unspoken cruel response would be:
"Stupid mother of a half-witted guy.
Just go home and wait for him; he'll show up.
Who would want to do anything with him?"

We must have been so innocent that we
Could not imagine odd circumstances
That someone would take advantage of him.

In an ordinary day at sunset,
We were standing at the corner of the street,
And wasting our time until we'd hear our mothers
Call asking us to come in for dinner.
Abraham's mother commingled with us.

This time she did not ask if we'd seen her son.
But uncharacteristically she started
To talk without expecting us to listen.

"Abraham is an old soul who was born
Too late to be able to intermix
With people and to meet their expectations.

"He was both satisfied and successful
When he was laboring hard at our farm,
Because he was free to do things his way.

"When he plowed, he sensed the oxen's fatigue.
Then stopped them at the middle of the furrow
To give them respite from the drudgery.
Then he hitched them when they were well recovered.
By treating his animals as his partner,
At the end of a laborious day,
He accomplished more than anyone else.

"When he milked the animals, he handled
Their udders with such a gentle manner
That they relaxed to let their milk flow freely,
So in no time his bucket overflowed.

"When he climbed up swaying trees to pick fruits,
In his hands ripened fruit did not get bruised.
When he reached to the higher branches,
He distributed his weight in a way
That thinner branches bent but did not break.

"He can comply well with natural laws,
Not with the rules of the society.

"Nowadays to get any work one has
To perform in line with a job description.
He can do things one way which is his way.
This approach makes him unemployable.

"All day long walking up and down to find
Something to do to make a few liras
Is not child's play; uncertainty exhausts.

"That's why I like him to come home early
So that he can recuperate to lead
One more day of a borderline life style."

At Hafiz's shop, Abraham stood behind
The bench and rocked while looking at the ceiling
As if he were not paying attention.
But when Hafiz needed another tool
He slapped that tool in his hand without saying
A word for there was no need for a word.

XII. My Mind Shifted to the Present

My mind shifted to the present and noticed
That the people were talking about Hafiz.

Levent stood up and said, "I might as well
Present myself no more than a stranger.
I left this Town a long time ago to
Find my good fortune but time passed me by.
I missed the birth days, then missed the death days;
Missed the fitful floods, missed the dreadful droughts."

When I returned for a short vacation,
I felt a peculiar anxiety.
In my mind, I reached the Town but no one
Would recognize me except Abraham.
And a poem was churning in my mind.

XIII. Unfulfilled Feelings

One may go, yet by chance he may never go back;
One may go back to find that lost ones leave no track.

While dreaming of back home, I start to fantasize
Since smoldering cinders of spent memories flare,
And soon consume themselves; then all at once they rise
From their ashes, like Phoenix, to take to the air.

It's easy to go back to that false paradise;
Why? Who's there to notice? Who's there to recognize?

Mainly, a final couplet kept whirling.

It's easy to go back to that false paradise;
Why? Who's there to notice? Who's there to recognize?

When I reached the Town, I felt much better.
To my surprise, I got in touch with friends.
Though Abraham was not at his old haunts,
I asked people about his whereabouts.
They said, "A child was just about to be
Smashed under the wheels of a speeding bus.
Abraham saved the child but lost his life."

Hafiz proclaimed Abraham as a martyr.
Thus, He became eligible to reach
Heaven without religious rituals.

In his pocket they found a small object
Which was wrapped in plastic and folded in
A triangular shape like an amulet.
They carefully peeled the worn-out covering
And found a barely legible poem.

XIV. Hear Me! The One Who Planned My Existence?

I

Each new day arrives without any certainty,
Though I've nothing to gain and nil to jeopardize.
I fantasize about having girls' company,
And then, I regret seeing the scorn in their eyes.

I made my debut not head first, but as a breech.
Life flaunts its goods, though there is zilch within my reach

II

I'm jailed into myself sans a chance of parole.
My desires and dreams are like an aborted twin.
Wayfarer! Proceed! Waste no prayers on my soul,
For I'm not given a chance to serve or to sin.

Here, I'm lost since my existence was not well planned.
Hereafter, God must guide me by holding my hand.

XV. Nurse Ayse

Nurse Ayse stood up and said, "When I was
A teenager, Hafiz used to come to our
House to process *bulgur* for our pantry.
I watched as he and his helper prepared
The work area at our patio.
He set his machine and then took his vest
Off and hung it on a hook on the wall
Without groping to find where that hook was.

I said, 'Uncle Hafiz, I hope you don't
Mind me asking a frivolous question.
I understand that you can operate
This machine for you have invented it.
What I like to know is a simple thing.
How did you know where the hook was located ?
He said, 'I have been in this house before.'

XVI. Secretary Sevim

Secretary Sevim said , "When I was
Young, I was visiting my Aunt who
Happened to be hosting Mrs. Hafiz.
They were reminiscing their honeymoons.

Mrs. Hafiz said, "It was a fine time.
Furthermore a time to learn and adjust.
One pleasant Sunday, Hafiz said, 'It would
Be fun to play hide-and-seek just like kids.
Furthermore, you'll have an edge over me.'

"I hid first, though he found me in no time;
Gave me a warm kiss and said, 'How could I
Miss your scent and the rhythm of your breathing?'"

"When he was to hide and I was to find,
I was feeling sympathetic with him,
And asking to myself, where a blind man
Can possibly hide during broad day light.

"Systematically, I search the bedrooms,
Bathrooms, living room, kitchen and basement.
To my surprise, he was not in those places.

"Our storeroom was damp, drafty and dreary,
And its high ceiling made it uninviting
I had to go down over rough stone steps
To get down on a polished tuff stone floor.

"Short distance from the entrance door, there was
A good sized pool to process grapes in autumn,
And a well to collect the fresh grape juice.
At other seasons pool was filled with goods.
In front of the walls there were walk-in bins
To store different kind of grains and flour.
There were huge amphorae which were scattered
All around to store food; besides, they were
Big enough for a man to hide inside.

"I searched inside and out but found no one.
I conceded defeat and asked him to
Come out of hiding; he said, 'Here I am.'
I lifted my head and saw him high up,
Smiling and sitting on a ceiling joist.

"After that my stereotypical
Understanding of disability
Completely changed, and so we built a life
Around our strength to raise our three daughters."

XVIII. Surveyor Salim

He stood up confidently and reported
An observation pertaining to Hafiz.

"He was a good friend with a family
Who happened to live across from my house.
When that family went on vacation,
He used to take care of their living things.
I used to see him walking down the street
With an excellent bodily posture,
Taking determined and regular steps.
When he'd come across from the neighbors' door,
He'd make a sharp right angle turn towards
The door and take out the key and insert
It into the key hole without groping.

"I am a surveyor, I know my directions;
It is impossible for a blind person
To do what he does so accurately.

"To satisfy my own curiosity,
I experimented with different
Methods of approaching his friend's front door.
I started from the main intersection,
And counted my steps to the target door.
Then I blindfolded myself and counted
My steps but each time I missed the target.
I excluded the possibilities
Of a hidden audible contraption,
Or a source that emits a special odor.

"I was relating to a friend of mine
That I was unable to solve Hafiz's
Skill to locate objects accurately.
He said, 'My Incredible tale might help.
My Grand Father was a veterinarian.
When Hafiz was a boy he found a bat
With a broken wing. He took it to my
Grandfather's office, and he set its wing.
Then Hafiz nursed it to a perfect health.
In return the bat taught echolocation
To Hafiz for him to find his way around'"

XVIII. Miner Mehmet

An old timer miner stood up and said,
"I spent all my working days under ground,
And I don't know what's claustrophobia.

"As it had happened many times before,
It was a normal warm day with blue skies,
Although Mt. Erciyes was completely
Covered with ominous looking dark clouds.

"Guessing what is next, we activated
Flood warning system, so people with their
Animals reached higher grounds, just in time
Before a slow moving flash flood rolled down.

"From the beginning that mixture of water,
Mud and pumice was over the banks
Of the Sandy Creek, and was running without
Hurry so that it could fill every barn,
Basement and business and carry away
What happened to be standing in its way.
It also flooded and silted the mosque,
And carried its veranda down the creek.

"Before there was the City of Develi,
There were the Seven Springs of Aquifer
Which were replenished by the Mt Erciyes.
Springs surfaced as a figure of Z.
They built a public fountain at each Source,
And the city grew around the fountains.

"Seyid Spring was unique for its fountain
Was not built, like others, where the Spring surfaced.
It bubbled at the bottom of a well,
Which was located long ways from a site,
Where were fountain could be built and it was
Accessible to the district's people.

"A long time ago they bored a tunnel
Through the bed rock which made it possible
For water to reach the site of the fountain.

"The location of the fountain was far
From being ideal for it was next
To the Sandy Creek which was prone to flooding.
At best, flooding made the fountain beyond reach,
And at worst it polluted the spring water.

"When the flood was over, people hurried
To the fountain; woefully, it was dry.
Hafiz and I deduced that a disaster
That could possibly happen did happen.
A mud and pumice mixture of the flood
Water and its pressure forced itself through
The access door of the tunnel and sealed
The eye of the Spring and plugged the tunnel.

"The underground passage was wide enough
For one man to labor productively.
We made a team of three: Hafiz, Abraham
And myself to open the plugged tunnel.
Darkness, dampness and tight working space meant
Nothing to us; when the lead man got tired
We rotated him to the back to give
Him less strenuous work to get some rest.

"Young men were more than willing to help us,
Although, they were out of their elements
In the dark and claustrophobic tunnel.
So we let them take away the debris
Which we were constantly producing.
They came in filled their wheelbarrows, and rushed
Toward the open space and bright sunshine.

"Midwife Zehra organized the ladies
According to age groups and formed two teams.
She assigned mature ones for the cleaning
Of the mosque where endless patience was needed
To dig the mud without tearing the rugs.

"She entrusted the cleaning of the fountain
To the young team for it required hard work.

"When calligrapher Kadir saw the zeal
Of the young team, he became motivated,
And returned with his brushes and paint tubes
To restore the faded inscription which
Was set above the high arch of the fountain.

"He painted the background into spring green,
And gilded the letters to give them life;
Also to make them clearly legible.

'Those who quench the thirst of souls, here and now,
Shall be served heavenly wine hereafter.'

"When we reached the bottom of the dry well,
To dig methodically, we divided
It into quadrants. Hafiz and Abraham
Stayed there; I went to the top of the well.
There district's people were speculating
About a future without their fountain.

"A brash adolescent boy was talking,
'These grown-up people are wasting their time.
There is not a Seyit Spring to be found.
It is backed up into the aquifer,
Now it's using its alternate channel.
Thus, it's united with the Saray Spring
And doubled the flow rate of that Spring.'

"An innocent girl was asking her father.
'Please Dad, tell to this big boy that he's wrong.
Our spring is longing for us and trying
To return for me to splash in its shallows.'

"Hafiz and Abraham were taking samples
From each quadrant and sending them up in
A bucket for me to assess their moisture.
I told them to dig deeper in to right upper
Quadrant which soon yielded muddy water.

"Everyone celebrated the occasion.
We let the Spring run free to clean itself.
After that we carefully scrubbed the tunnel.
Hafiz built a new door for the tunnel's entrance
Which was as sturdy as a castle door.

"When the water became perfectly pure,
Folks gathered at the fountain to celebrate.
Hafiz filled the bottles of the babies
And the glasses of all and blessed them all.

"After that I retired for the last time
For all my reserve energy was drained.

"In the late afternoons, as I'd be going
To teahouse to play backgammon with friends,
I watched Abraham and Hafiz building
The west wall of Hafiz's house which was
Ruined by the flood, but he would not take time
To rebuild his own residence, before
The public fountain project was completed.
Abraham was handing the stones and Hafiz
Was laying them without space between them."

XIX. Policeman Ziya

Ziya stood up and said, "My uncle was
A zaptiah during the World War I.
A group of minority men were building
Bombs and stock piling war weapons to use
Against the Turkish people of the town.

"Develi was under both martial law
And a curfew from sunset to sunrise.
One evening my uncle and his fellow
Officers were making their routine rounds.

"They heard loud noises coming from a store.
Although, no light could be seen from outside.
They thought somebody camouflaged the store,
In order to build something illegal.
They ordered that the door must be opened.

"When the door was opened officers asked
Hafiz to turn the lights on so they could
See what was going on. He said, 'I have
No lights to turn on for I'm a blind man.
To make ends meet, I'm building furniture.
My night labor pays as well as day labor.'

"They asked if he needed help to go home.
He said, 'All I desire is the freedom
To labor at any hour of the day.'
Officers issued a permanent pass."

"I've a few pieces of his furniture
Which are simple, sturdy and beautiful."

XX. Locksmith Garabet

Garabet stood up and said, "Develi
Isn't a lucrative place for locksmiths.
Yes, there are many historic buildings
With huge locks and keys unlike modern ones.
While repairing them one has to go into
The mind of the original craftsman:
One must have talent, skill, patience and time.

"After working on a handful of them,
I started to refer those time consuming
Problems to Hafiz, for I could not charge
Enough for my time to make a living.
Today's locks and keys are not challenging
However, they put the bread on the table.

"Somehow Hafiz had enough time and skill
To preserve something unique from the past.
If somebody were not to repair those
Rusty relics, then we'll have to replace
Them with shiny new locks with tiny keys."

XXI. Doctor Fahri Bey

Doctor Fahri stood up and said, "Hafiz
Never came to my office for a checkup
Or consultation; however, I went
To his shop to talk about the recent
Progress that is made in diagnostic
And in surgical ophthalmology.

"I reminded him that in the old-times
He'd no valid diagnostic workup.

"A good friend of mine is a professor
Of ophthalmology in a hospital
Of the University of Istanbul.

"They're performing delicate surgeries
On all parts of the eye, including lens,
Retina and doing corneal transplants.

"I said, I'll make all the appointments
And take time off to accompany him.

"He thanked and said, 'You are a blessed healer.
You see someone who is lacking something,
And instantly you try to make him whole.
However, the way I see, my blindness
Is not a curse; it's a blessing of God.
By being blind, I did not see the face
Of fear, anger, hatred and ugliness.
And yet, I can feel the peace, contentment
And beauty for they're the space I live in.'"

XXII. Ince Zade

Imam of Aloglu Mosque stood up and
Said, "When I was asked to be the imam
And fill the vacancy left by Hafiz,
I had a difficult time to decide,
For there was an ethical violation.

"Years ago elders of the mosque hired him,
Both as an imam and a muezzin.
They surely knew that he was a blind man.
He performed his duties diligently,
And was respected by his congregation.

"At the time of Jesus, people who had
Visible disabilities would not
Be allowed to go into the Temple.

"A pack of fundamentalist elders
Came to power and they searched old treatise,
And found nebulous clauses which did not
Endorse praying behind a blind imam.

"I told Hafiz, what they have done to you
Is sinful and against the civil laws.
I said , I'll organize your congregation
And fight until we get you reinstated.

"'He said, 'I don't want to cause any trouble
To anyone, I'll turn the other cheek.'"

"He continued to attend prayers, five
Times a day, which were conducted by me.

"While an imam leads a prayer, he must
Recite the words as they are in the Book.
In case he skips a word, it's the duty
Of the worshippers to speak up the missing
Word and then imam must repeat it.

"Most corrections came from Hafiz for he
Had the best photographic memory."

XXIII. Banker Bekir

Banker Bekir stood up and said, "Hafiz
Lends money without any interest,
To his needy neighbors, friends and relatives.

"When he was younger he'd not keep any
Record of the transactions, when he grew
Older, he'd write on a piece of paper
Who owed what which had no legal standing.

I said, "I know you don't charge interest
Because it is against religious laws.
However, inflation is eating up
Your principal; therefore it is halal
To adjust their debt in line with inflation.

Hafiz said, 'For a banker what you suggest
Makes a good sense, if not, you go bankrupt.
You don't see my clientele in your bank,
For they don't qualify for a bank loan.
However, what they may lack in resources,
They compensate with dependability.
Thus far no one is behind of his payment.'

Closing Words of Hafiz

1.
Let's celebrate this day for it's a gift;
If not, no one can earn it or keep it.
Peace and love for all.

2.
Gratitude to our neighbors and townsmen,
Since they expand the family circle.
Peace and love for all.

3.
Gratitude to *The One* who empowered
And trusted us with 'A Couple of Words.'
We'll realize how big this favor is
When we remember that there was *The Word*
Before there was anything but *The Void*.

God fashioned this world with a single word.
He said, 'Be!' and the universes were.

We must perceive that words are an effective
Tool on our tongue which can lift one's spirit
Or wound in a way that it will not heal.

A soft whisper starts a sweet love affair:
An unintentional word turns it sour.

I do not like to speak malicious words.
I even like to deny their existence,
However, left alone they are capable
Of flowing and fouling the public well.
Peace and love for all.

4.
Gratitude to the space: endless expanse
Which contains the universes and their
Countless galaxies with billions of stars,
Yet nothing can fill up its spaciousness.

The endlessness of the space is not emptiness.
Stars are born and die in there and their remains
Are voraciously consumed by black holes.
Then black holes disappear; still space lives on.

It's clear to see the sound economy,
And the order of The Universe where
Nothing is wasted but all is recycled.

When one thinks all things are under control,
Cosmic expansion is accelerated
By inexplicable dark energy.

There are too many veiled things we can't see,
Thus we're blessed for everything we can't see.
Peace and love for all.

5.

Gratitude to the *Planet Earth* for being
Located at an optimal distance
From The Sun's life providing energy.

The Earth did not just bask under *The Sun*.
It exposed its atmosphere and water
To Sun's rays to germinate life on Earth.

All through eons *The Earth* is evolving.
The Arctic ice and ocean streams have their roles.
What's more, under different circumstances,
It had proper places for lives to prosper.

Deserts foster their cacti and sidewinders.
Marshlands have their fish, birds and crocodiles.
Placid pastures nurture their lambs and wolves.
The Earth embraces all its living things.

Compared to *The Cosmos*, The Earth's a speck.
For us, without that speck, Cosmos is worthless.
Peace and love for all.

6.

Gratitude to our courage to let go
Our enslaving compulsions and attachments
To allow ourselves to love and live freely.
Though genuine freedom is elusive,
Since the ghosts of habits lust to lurk back.

When we desire to know good things, we should
Remember *The Creator* of good things.
Peace and love for all.

7.

Gratitude to our sober side to reason,
And to our whimsical nature for finding
Time to dream in an absorbing workday:

To our intrinsic resilience to heal
After being stunned with an awful blow;

To our human power of starting over
When we feel we can no longer go forward.
Peace and love for all.

8.

Gratitude to human determination
To seek after the elusive truth while
Simple superstitions can satisfy us.

And to our altruistic potential
To love all living things without expecting
Personal gain or glory in return.
Peace and love for all.